# BLACK WIDOW SPIDER

**Written by**
William Anthony

GROSS
LIFE
CYCLES

©2021
BookLife Publishing Ltd.
King's Lynn
Norfolk PE30 4LS

ISBN: 978-1-83927-480-0

**Written by:**
William Anthony

**Edited by:**
Emilie Dufresne

**Designed by:**
Amy Li

# BLACK WIDOW SPIDER

| Page 4 | What Is a Life Cycle? |
| Page 5 | Gross Life Cycles |
| Page 6 | What Is a Black Widow Spider? |
| Page 8 | Egg Cases |
| Page 10 | Spiderlings |
| Page 12 | A Sticky Situation |
| Page 14 | Mealtime |
| Page 16 | End of the Road |
| Page 18 | A Gross Life |
| Page 22 | Gross Life Cycle of a Black Widow Spider |
| Page 23 | Get Exploring! |
| Page 24 | Glossary and Index |

Words that look like **this** can be found in the glossary on page 24.

# WHAT IS A LIFE CYCLE?

All animals, plants and humans go through different stages of their life as they grow and change. This is called a life cycle.

**Human life cycle**

 **Baby** →  **Child** → **Adult**

4

# GROSS LIFE CYCLES

All life cycles are different. They can be quick or slow. They can have lots of steps or not many at all. Did you know that some can also be totally GROSS?

Life cycles can be freaky, scary and full of smelly splats. Gross!

# WHAT IS A BLACK WIDOW SPIDER?

A black widow spider is a type of **arachnid**. Just like other spiders, black widow spiders have eight legs and you might find them sitting on a **web**.

Can you count all eight legs?

6

Black widow spiders have a scary, gross life cycle. There is a lot of biting, chewing and churning. It has a horrible ending too...

7

# EGG CASES

Female black widows have a red mark. Can you see it?

A black widow spider starts its life cycle as an egg. Spider eggs are laid by adult female spiders.

A female black widow will lay hundreds of eggs at the same time. She then wraps them in a case made of **silk** to keep them safe.

Spiders make silk inside their bodies. Some use it to make webs.

# SPIDERLINGS

Soon after, baby spiders will **hatch** from the eggs. Baby spiders are called spiderlings. After they hatch, the spiderlings will break out of the egg case.

Hundreds of little spiderlings will come from this egg case.

Not many spiderlings survive to become an adult like this.

When the spiderlings hatch, they are so hungry that they often eat their own brothers and sisters! How gross! 11

# A STICKY SITUATION

It's time to find a new home. The spiderling shoots out a sticky blob of silk. The silk carries the spiderling in the wind to its next home.

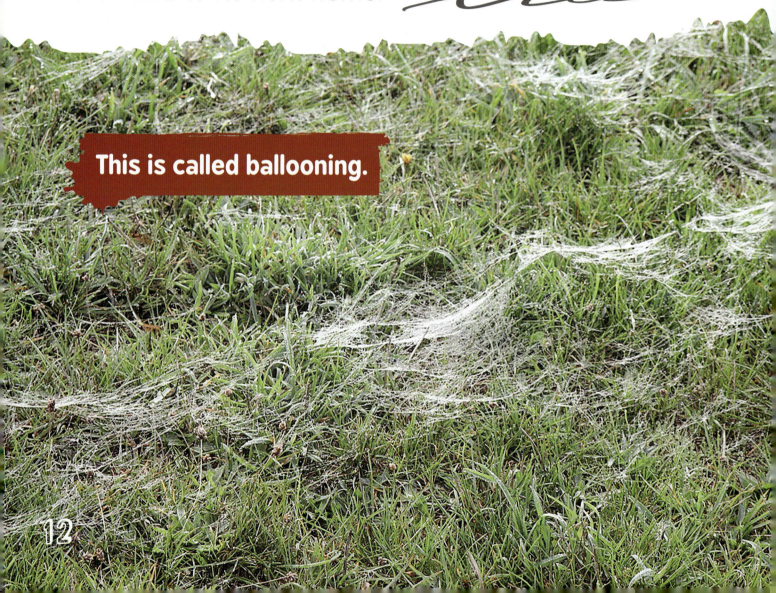

This is called ballooning.

Black widow spiders often have messy webs.

When it is ready, the spiderling will make its first web. The web is made of very sticky silk. Lots of **insects** can get trapped in it. The spider will then eat those insects. 13

# MEALTIME

Female black widow spider

Male black widow spider

Mating needs one female spider and one male spider.

. When the black widow spider has grown into an adult, it looks for a mate. Mates are two animals of the same kind that can make babies together.

14

Once the female black widow has mated with the male, she may do something horrible. She may gobble him up! This helps the eggs to grow inside the female.

# END OF THE ROAD

When she is ready, the female black widow will lay her eggs. This starts the life cycle all over again.

Black widow spiders often live for around one year.
However, some black widow spiders may live for
up to three years.

# A GROSS LIFE

Black widow spiders do other gross things too. They have **fangs** that they can use to bite other animals, including humans!

When a black widow spider bites something, it passes **venom** through its fangs. That venom can make us very ill.

Never touch a spider that looks like this!

A black widow bite can make our bodies **ache** and hurt. A bite might also make it difficult to breathe.

Don't worry, a black widow spider will not bite you
if you keep away from it. Black widow spiders only
bite when they are scared!

21

# GROSS LIFE CYCLE OF A BLACK WIDOW SPIDER

**1** A female black widow lays eggs.

**2** Spiderlings hatch and eat each other.

GROSS LIFE CYCLES

**3** Spiderlings make their webs and catch food.

**4** Adult black widows mate and the female may eat the male.

# GET EXPLORING!

There are lots of different types of spider. When you go outside, see how many spider webs you can find. Make sure you do not touch any of the webs!

# GLOSSARY

**ache**      a type of pain that can continue for a long time

**arachnid**    a type of animal that has eight legs, such as spiders and scorpions

**fangs**      long, sharp teeth

**hatch**      when a baby animal comes out of its egg

**insects**     animals with one or two pairs of wings, six legs and no backbone

**silk**      the thin thread that is made by a spider

**venom**     a harmful thing that is injected through a bite or a sting

**web**      a net made from silk threads put together by a spider

# INDEX

**adults** 4, 8, 14, 22
**bites** 18–21
**eggs** 8–10, 15–16, 22
**insects** 13
**legs** 6

**mating** 14–15, 22
**silk** 9, 12–13
**spiderlings** 10–13, 22
**webs** 6, 13, 22–23

**PHOTO CREDITS**   Images are courtesy of Shutterstock.com. With thanks to Getty Images, Thinkstock Photo and iStockphoto.

Recurring images – Milan M (grunge shapes), Sonechko57 (splat shapes), Jojje, Infinity32829 (paper background), Rimma Z (watercolour splatters), Sopelkin, Chinch, Ermak Oksana (decorative vectors). Cover–p1 – Protasov AN, nikiteev_konstantin, p2–3 – iSKYDANCER, Matteo photos, p4–5 – Gelpi, ANURAK PONGPATIMET, elwynn, wong sze yuen, p6–7 –Jay Ondreicka, Nate Allred, p8–9 – Viktor Loki, Jeff W. Jarrett, p10–11 – Jacobo Quero, Jeff W. Jarrett, p12–13 – Meister Photos, Stephen Michael Barnett (wiki commons), p14–15 – Malpolon, lighTTrace Studio, p16–17– Paula Cobleigh, Don Bendickson, p18–19 – TY Lim, Pong Wira, p20–21 – Riccardo Mayer, CGN089, p22–23 – lighTTrace Studio, Jeff W. Jarrett, Matteo photos, Meister Photos, Tom Wang.